Nine True Dolphin Stories

by MARGARET DAVIDSON

Illustrated by ROGER WILSON

SCHOLASTIC BOOK SERVICES
NEW YORK · TORONTO · LONDON · AUCKLAND · SYDNEY · TOKYO

ISBN: 0-590-03058-2

Text copyright © 1974 by Margaret Davidson. Illustrations copyright © 1974 by Scholastic Magazines, Inc. All rights reserved. Published by Scholastic Book Services, a division of Scholastic Magazines, Inc.

15 14 13 12 11 10 9 8 7 6

01/8

Printed in the U.S.A.

02

Dolphins look like fish. They live their whole lives where fish live. But they are not fish. They are mammals — just like you and me.

That is why dolphins come to the top of the water so often. Like all mammals, they must breathe air. Some people say dolphins come to the top of the water for another reason too. To see what's going on.

Most dolphins, like most people, are very curious. They are interested in everything around them. Dolphins seem to be like people in other ways too. Some are shy. Some are big show-offs. Some are bright. Some are a little slow to learn. Some are very friendly and like to swim with many other dolphins. Some are happiest when they are swimming alone.

There are many different dolphins. And there are many different stories to tell — all of them true.

Contents

The Story of Pelorus Jack,
the faithful dolphin

The country of New Zealand is made up of two main islands. Between them is a big body of water called Cook Strait. One summer day in 1888 a steamship was going through those waters, carrying passengers from one island to another. Suddenly a dolphin came to the top of the water. He swam with the ship for miles. Sometimes he swam by the side of the ship. Sometimes he swam in front of it. Then, with a flick of his tail, he was gone.

But the next day the dolphin was back. And the next, and the next—always swimming with one ship or another. But at the end of the day the dolphin would swim away. He would swim into a small inlet of water called Pelorus Bay. Before long, people began to call the dolphin Pelorus Jack.

The waters of Cook Strait were full of fast currents, jagged rocks, and even

whirlpools. Some people thought that Pelorus Jack had decided to act as a pilot. They said he was showing the ship where it was safe to go.

"Nonsense!" other people said. "He's just having a good time."

Whatever the reason, more and more people began to ride the ships. They all wanted to see the dolphin. They would crowd close to the railings and peer out across the choppy water of Cook Strait. "Here comes Jack!" someone would cry as the dolphin raced toward the boat.

Jack became more and more famous. People wrote about him in magazines and newspapers. His picture was printed on postcards. A chocolate candy was named after him. And people came from far away to see the dolphin who swam with ships.

The sailors on these steamships had a special feeling for Jack. He brought them good luck, they said. As long as Pelorus Jack swam with their ship, nothing could go wrong. And nothing bad would ever happen to Jack either, the sailors said — not if they could help it.

But one day Jack was swimming with a ship named the *S.S. Penguin.* As usual, the railing high above the water was crowded with people laughing and talking and pointing at Jack. One young man was standing apart. Now he slowly raised a gun —and fired it at Jack!

The bullet whizzed through the air. It missed. But Jack dived deep in the water and sped away. From that day on, Pelorus Jack would not go near the *Penguin*.

Before long the sailors began to call the *Penguin* a bad-luck ship. One sailor would not work on her anymore. "Jack won't have anything to do with her," he said. "Why should I?"

Now people began to worry about Jack. One man had already taken a shot at him. What was to stop another? Jack's many friends decided that a law should be passed to protect him. In 1904 the New Zealand government agreed. From then on it was against the law for anyone to harm Pelorus Jack in any way. This was the first law in history written especially to protect a dolphin.

For the next few years Pelorus Jack went on swimming with the ships. Then, in the summer of 1912, four Norwegian whaling boats sailed into Cook Strait. They were supposed to hunt only the big whales.

But a few days later Jack didn't show up. He didn't come around the next day, or the next. People on the ships would stare out over the water. They would think they saw something speeding toward them. "Here comes Jack!" they would cry. But their eyes —or their hearts—were playing tricks on them. Pelorus Jack was never seen again.

What had happened? Had Jack decided to go somewhere else? No one who knew the faithful dolphin could believe that. Maybe he had died of old age. Jack had been swimming with ships for twenty-two years. That is old for a dolphin.

But many of Jack's friends feared something else. They feared that one of the whaling boats had captured him—and boiled him down for oil!

Was this true? No one would ever know for sure. But a newspaper printed a story about Pelorus Jack's life. And it summed up everyone's feelings very well. The story ended: "If he is dead, more's the pity. If he has been slaughtered, more's the shame!"

The Story of Opo,
the dolphin who loved people

Pelorus Jack loved ships. But he was a wild dolphin. In all the years he swam with ships he never let a person touch him.

Opo was different. She was a wild dolphin too. But she tamed herself. She liked to be close to people.

Opononi, New Zealand, was a quiet little town by the sea. Most of the men worked as fishermen. In the summer of 1955, they noticed that a strange sea animal was following their boats. At first the men thought it must be a shark. But the animal came closer and closer to the boats. And before long everyone could see it was a dolphin. One of the fishermen named her Opo—after the town.

At first Opo was shy, as many wild dolphins are. But she was curious too. Every day she swam closer to the boats. Finally one of the fishermen reached out as far as he could with his oar. He scratched Opo with it.

She reared back in the water. But the oar must have felt good. For soon Opo came closer than ever before. Then she rolled over. The men had to laugh. For Opo was plainly saying "Scratch my belly, this time."

Opo swam alongside all kinds of boats. But she liked motorboats best. "She had a real weakness for the sound of an outboard motor," a fisherman said. "She would follow a motorboat just like a dog on a leash."

One evening Opo followed a motorboat all the way back to the town dock. From that day on she spent more and more time near the shore.

A scientist came to look at Opo. He said she was a young dolphin. Probably she had lost her mother. That was why she was swimming alone. Opo might be an orphan, but she soon found a new family. The whole town of Opononi adopted the friendly dolphin.

Near the town dock was a sandy beach. Opo spent most of her time swimming there. At first she would dart away if anyone came too near. But before long she would swim with anyone who was gentle. She even let them touch her sometimes.

Opo liked children best of all. "I have seen her swimming among children almost begging to be petted," a woman remembers. Sometimes a child would stand in the water with his legs apart. Then Opo would swim under him, pick him up, and take him for a short ride on her back.

One day someone gave Opo a beach ball. She loved that ball! She balanced it on her flippers. She bounced it high in the air.

She let it roll down her back and swatted it hard with her tail.

The townspeople often stopped to watch Opo playing in the water. When she did something especially exciting they would cheer and clap. Then Opo would leap high in the air again and again. Opo, the once shy dolphin, had become a dolphin show-off. But she was careful never to leap when people were swimming nearby. She was always gentle with her human friends.

Before long news of Opo got around. More and more people began to make special trips to see the dolphin. Weekends were especially busy. There was only one hotel in town. And every room was rented. Every space in the nearby campground was filled. And still more people came.

The one road that ran through town was

often jammed with cars and trucks. The beach was packed with people. They all wanted to see Opo. Some people wanted to touch her so much they waded into the water with their clothes on.

The town was often very crowded. But the townspeople didn't mind. For this was a special kind of crowd. The gentle dolphin seemed to have the same effect on everyone. No one argued. No one got drunk. In the evening when it was too cold and dark to visit Opo, people sat around in small friendly groups and talked about her.

The townspeople of Opononi were happy to share Opo with others. But they had one worry. Someone had tried to shoot another dolphin, Pelorus Jack. What if that happened to Opo?

The people put up a sign on the edge of

town — warning others not to shoot the dolphin. But a sign is only made of wood and words. What if words weren't enough? A law had been passed to protect Pelorus Jack. All over New Zealand people began to ask for a law to protect Opo.

In March of 1956 a special law was passed to protect her. But on that very same day Opo did not come near the shore. She did not come to swim with the boats. She did not come to play with her human friends.

That first day no one worried very much. Opo had gone off on her own before, for a few hours at a time. But the next morning came — and still no Opo. Now people began to worry.

Four boats searched the harbor from end to end. But they found no sign of Opo. "She'll come back," the children said. *Please tell us she'll be back*, was what they really meant.

But Opo didn't come back — alive. The next morning a fisherman found her body caught on some rocks. Somehow she had stranded herself. No one ever knew why.

That evening Opo's body was brought back to the beach where she had played so happily. The next day she was buried beside the town hall. Her grave was covered with flowers. Almost everyone in town came to that funeral. Some stood sad and silent. Many were crying.

"I'll never forget her," one girl sobbed.

"Of course not," her mother answered. "None of us will."

And it was true. The friendly dolphin had come and made them happy. The people of Opononi would remember her forever.

Opo tamed herself. She loved people. But most wild dolphins are far too shy to come close to shore. So no one knew very much about them.

Then a group of men had a wonderful idea. They couldn't live where dolphins live. They couldn't live in the sea. So they brought the sea up onto dry land.

They built a big tank in the ground and filled it with salt water. In this tank they put many different sea animals — shrimp, seahorses, lobsters, dragon fish, turtles, eels, and of course dolphins. The tank was really a little bit of ocean up on dry land. So the men called it an *oceanarium*. It opened in 1938. This very first oceanarium in the world was named Marineland of Florida.

The Story of Spray,
the first dolphin born in a tank

One spring morning in 1947 a man stood by the tank at Marineland. He leaned forward and stared at one of the dolphins. Then he turned and shouted. "Hey! Come quick! Mona's having her baby!"

People came running from all directions. For this was a very special moment. The first baby dolphin in a tank was about to be born.

People weren't the only ones to be interested. In the tank the other dolphins formed a tight circle around Mona. Perhaps they were curious too. But there was another reason for gathering around.

Dolphins do not have enemies in the tank. But they do have enemies in the sea. Killer whales are their enemies. And so are sharks. A newborn baby dolphin is only three feet long. It would make a very tasty snack for a hungry whale or shark. So all the other dolphins were protecting the mother and her child.

"Look!" cried one of the men. The baby was being born. First her tail appeared. Then her belly. And finally her head. She was born tail first — as all dolphins are. The men named her Spray.

As soon as Spray entered her world of water she had a job to do. And she had to do it fast. She had to swim to the top of the tank for her first breath of air.

She wriggled her tail at double speed and got to the top by herself. But later, people learned that sometimes a baby is too weak to make that first swim by itself. Or it swims in the wrong direction. Down! It's in no danger, though. The mother dolphin is right there. She swims under her baby, and bumps the slowpoke up for its first breath of air.

Some animals are almost helpless at birth. Puppies are. So are kittens. But not dolphins. From the very first, Spray could see. She could hear. She could swim. She could even "talk" to her mother. The little dolphin made a whistling sound through her blowhole. And Mona whistled right back.

Spray could do all sorts of things that big dolphins do. But she couldn't eat fish. She had no teeth. That was all right. She didn't need them. Not yet. For many months she would drink her mother's milk.

Spray was too young to eat fish. But one day she found a piece of fish in the water and began to play with it. She swallowed it by mistake. Poor Spray! Her stomach wasn't ready for fish. It was plain that she had a terrible stomachache. But Mona knew just what to do. She rubbed and rubbed Spray's belly with her flipper. Finally Spray gave a little burp and felt better again.

Spray ate under water. And she slept there too. But she could never sleep for long, because she had to come up for air. So she took catnaps instead. Sometimes she would close both eyes. But often she slept with only one closed — the one on the outside. She kept her other eye wide open. Then she could watch her mother.

Mona kept an eye on Spray too. At first this was easy. During the first few weeks Spray stuck to her mother's side like a small shadow. But finally she began to try swimming away. There were so many things in the tank to see and taste and smell!

Mona never let her get far. Spray would swim a few feet. Then Mona would nudge her back again. But Spray was growing up. Each day she grew bigger — and bolder.

She swam farther and farther away. For a long time Mona was patient. She would swim after Spray and bring her back again and again. But finally Mona ran out of patience. One day she punished Spray — dolphin style.

She pushed Spray down to the bottom of the tank and sat on her for thirty seconds

or so! Did the punishment work? It certainly did. For hours afterward Spray was a *very* quiet, *very* well-behaved dolphin.

Mona was a careful mother. But she knew when it was time to let Spray start taking care of herself. By the time Spray was six months old, she had teeth. Now she could eat fish — without getting a stomachache.

By the time Spray was a year old, she was almost as big as the other dolphins in the tank. It was time for her to live on her own. But whenever she felt tired or lonely or scared she would swim right back to Mona's side. Spray was a grown-up dolphin. But she and her mother remained the best of friends.

The Story of Pauline,
the dolphin who almost died of loneliness

One day some men from an oceanarium sailed out to sea. They were looking for dolphins. And they caught one they named Pauline.

As soon as they slipped Pauline into the tank, the men knew something was wrong. She couldn't — or wouldn't — swim. She would sink to the bottom of the tank. The doctor examined her. But he could find nothing wrong. "She'll probably be all right when she gets used to the tank," he said.

But meanwhile Pauline had to breathe. How could they keep her from sinking to the bottom? The men wove some ropes together and made a raft for her. At each corner of the raft they tied a big glass jar so the raft wouldn't sink. Then they slid Pauline on top of the raft.

Poor Pauline. For two days she drifted around the tank on her raft. She could breathe. But she would not eat. Sometimes she whistled a high sharp whistle. This was Pauline's distress whistle. It was her way of crying "help!". But nobody answered her cry. Nobody whistled back.

Once more the doctor examined her. "I still don't know what is wrong," he said. "But I do know one thing. If she doesn't begin eating soon, she'll die."

On the third day the men sailed out to

sea again. They caught another dolphin and slipped him into the tank. Pauline didn't even see him. She was drifting around with her eyes closed. But a few minutes later she happened to whistle. It was a very low whistle — a whisper of a whistle of distress.

But someone whistled back! Pauline's eyes

popped open! She whistled again. And the new dolphin swam over to her side. He nudged her head gently. Then he began to drift around the tank with her.

"Look!" cried one of the men. Pauline was moving her flippers. Her tail was beginning to beat up and down. Pauline was trying to swim!

The men slid Pauline off the raft. Very slowly she began to move around the tank. Once or twice she started to sink in the water. But the new dolphin just swam down and pushed her back up again.

Before the day was over Pauline began to eat. The next morning the men could hardly believe their eyes. There was Pauline — the dolphin who had almost died of loneliness — playing a fast game of water-tag with her new friend.

The Story of Bimbo,
the big bully

Bimbo was a pilot whale. He was one of the first pilot whales to live in a tank. (Pilot whales and dolphins are closely related. Most scientists say that pilot whales are really a kind of big dolphin. They are both members of the toothed whale family.)

For months Bimbo lived happily with a group of dolphins in an oceanarium near Los Angeles, California. Then one day — no one ever knew why — Bimbo stopped being friendly. Bimbo became a bully instead.

He began to pick on the dolphins in the tank, especially the baby dolphins. Bimbo was a full-grown pilot whale. He weighed almost two thousand pounds. Now he was a very dangerous bully.

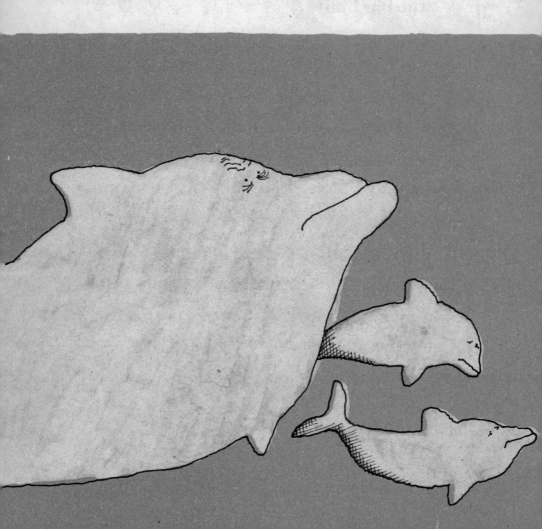

Something had to be done. But what? The director of the oceanarium worked out a plan. "It's an experiment," he said. "I hope it works."

He gave an order. One of the workers opened a valve near the bottom of the tank. Slowly the water began to drain out. The tank was drained until there was only three feet of water left in it. This didn't bother the dolphins at all. They could still swim freely in three feet of water.

But not Bimbo! He was too big. Now he was stuck — half in and half out of the water. Bimbo began to whistle the sharp high whistle of distress. "I'm in trouble! Somebody help!"

The dolphins had every reason to be angry with Bimbo. But as soon as they heard that whistle they swam right over.

They gathered around Bimbo and began to whistle too. Their whistles were soft and gentle. "Don't worry. Nothing's going to happen to you. We're here," they seemed to be saying.

Bimbo seemed to be listening too. Finally he stopped crying. He still didn't look happy. But he didn't seem so afraid.

The director was standing nearby. Now he gave a signal, and water began to enter the tank. Soon it was back to its old level. Bimbo could swim once more.

Did the experiment work? It certainly did. Bimbo must have remembered those minutes of terror — and the kindness of the dolphins. Now his bullying days were over. He never picked on anyone again.

The Story of Flippy,
the first trained dolphin

Today there are many dolphin shows
in the United States. People come from
far away to watch dolphins do all kinds of
wonderful tricks. But once, not very long
ago, there were no trained dolphins at all.

It all began at the first oceanarium,
Marineland of Florida. Dolphins had been
living in the tank there for more than ten
years. Again and again men had watched

them make up many difficult games and tricks. What could dolphins do if they were *really* trained? The men of Marineland decided to find out.

Who would they get to train the very first dolphin? "We need someone who has trained other animals," the director said. Where would they find such a man? At a circus, of course!

The director of Marineland wrote to Ringling Brothers Circus. Soon a letter came from Ringling Brothers. One of their best trainers, it said, was a man named Adolf Frohn. He had trained all kinds of animals — sea lions, seals, raccoons, rabbits, white rats, doves, and many others. In 1950 Adolf Frohn came to Marineland to add a dolphin to his list.

The dolphin's name was Flippy. Mr.

Frohn stood at the edge of the tank and watched Flippy. What kind of things should he try to teach him? "A kangaroo I teach jumping tricks," Adolf Frohn thought. "A flea I teach to hop. All right. Dolphins like to leap, catch things, and swim very fast. I will work on this."

He decided he would try to teach Flippy to jump through a hoop held high in the air. But how could he get Flippy to do it? Mr. Frohn was a very experienced animal trainer. He knew that the answer was, *one step at a time*.

First Mr. Frohn stretched a net across the shallow end of the tank. He stood on one side of the net. Flippy swam on the other. Mr. Frohn held up a big piece of fish. "Come, Flippy! Jump!" he called loudly.

For days Flippy just swam round and

round on his side of the net. But he wanted that fish! So one morning when Mr. Frohn said, "Come, Flippy! Jump!" Flippy jumped over the net. "Good boy, Flippy!" Adolf Frohn said. And gave Flippy his first reward.

Next Mr. Frohn took away the net. He put a rope in its place. Flippy leaped over the rope right away. Little by little Mr. Frohn raised the rope in the air. And Flippy kept on jumping. Every time he jumped over the rope Mr. Frohn praised him — and gave him a piece of fish. Finally the rope was ten feet in the air. And Flippy was still jumping.

But one day Mr. Frohn took the rope away. He held a big hoop in its place. Flippy took one look at that hoop and started to swim in the other direction! Flippy, like most dolphins, hated to go through anything small.

"Come, Flippy! Jump!" Mr. Frohn said again and again. Each time, Flippy turned tail and swam away. But Mr. Frohn was very patient. And Flippy had grown to trust his human friend. Finally Flippy jumped high out of the water and sailed through the hoop.

"Well done!" cried Adolf Frohn. Flippy had learned his first trick.

In the next few months the dolphin learned many more tricks. Flippy learned to roll over and over in the water, to catch a rubber ball, ring a gong, honk a horn, raise a flag, and jump through a paper-covered hoop. He learned to shake hands with his flippers, put out fires with his tail, take bows, dance backwards, and "sing" by

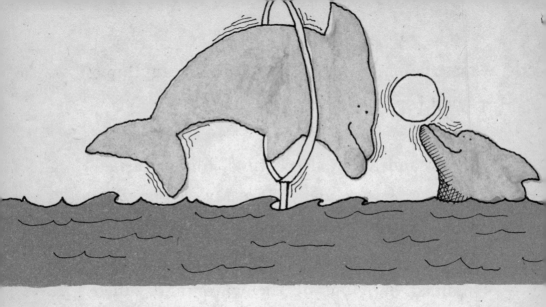

making a wailing sound through his blowhole. He played basketball, baseball, and football. He even learned to bowl.

Flippy learned all these things from Adolf Frohn. And Adolf Frohn learned some very interesting things from Flippy too:

He learned that a dolphin will not work for someone he doesn't like. So before you teach a dolphin anything, you must become his friend.

When a dolphin does something right, you must give him a reward. The best rewards are simple ones — a few words of praise and a piece of fish.

You must never, never bully a dolphin. "You will never get anywhere with a dolphin by force," Adolf Frohn explained. "If you try to punish him he will swim to the far corner of the tank. He will not pay any attention to you. If you keep on, he will go on a hunger strike. A dolphin will even let himself die rather than do something he doesn't want to do."

Often dolphins will work without a fish reward. Many times Flippy did his whole act without swallowing a single piece of fish. He worked for the fun of it.

The tricks must be hard enough to be interesting. Many animals are happy to do the same simple trick again and again. But not dolphins. They get bored. When a dolphin gets bored, he may go on strike. Then you can offer him a whole bucketful of fish, and he still won't work.

Dolphins are good students. They are good teachers too. A dolphin will learn a trick. Then he will teach it to all the other dolphins in his tank.

Adolf Frohn learned many things about dolphins. Most important, he learned that dolphins are very, very smart. "I have worked with many animals," he said. "No other animal learns so quickly, and forgets so little."

For almost a year Mr. Frohn taught Flippy. Finally he decided Flippy was ready to do his tricks in public. It was time for the first dolphin show.

People crowded around the tank to watch. They *oohed* and *ahhed* and clapped as Mr. Frohn led Flippy through one trick after another. "You know," said someone standing nearby, "if that dolphin gets any smarter he'll be talking soon."

Adolf Frohn smiled. "Oh, he does talk," he answered. *"We're* just too dumb to understand him!"

The Story of Doris and Buzz,
the dolphins who talked to each other

Dolphins make many kinds of sounds. They squeak, squawk, squeal, mew, rasp, click, and clack. When they are upset or excited they even yelp like dogs. Most of all they whistle.

But is this really *talking* — the way people talk? Are they really passing information to each other? Or are they only sharing simple feelings and fears — the way other animals like cats and dogs do?

A scientist named Dr. Jarvis Bastian decided to find out. He worked with two dolphins named Doris and Buzz in a tank at the University of California.

Dr. Bastian placed four buttons under water. Two buttons were for Doris. Two were for Buzz. Then he got an old auto headlight. This was his signal. Sometimes Dr. Bastian turned on the headlight and let it shine steadily. This meant "push the right-hand button." Sometimes he let the headlight blink on and off. Then Doris and Buzz were supposed to push their left-hand button instead.

Before long Doris and Buzz learned to watch the light. They pushed down the correct button with their snouts. Then Dr. Bastian gave them their reward — a piece of fish.

He made the experiment harder. The dolphins still had to watch the headlight and push down the correct button. But now Doris had to wait. Buzz had to push his button down first. *Then* it was Doris's turn. If she pushed her button first, neither dolphin got any fish.

At first Doris and Buzz made a few mistakes. But soon they learned how to do this too. Now it was time for the last and most important part of the experiment.

Dr. Bastian put a wooden wall across the pool. Doris and her two buttons were on one side of the wall. Buzz and his two buttons were on the other side. *But only Doris could see the headlight.* Only she could see if it was shining steadily, or blinking. Only she could see what the signal was. But Doris had to wait for Buzz to press his button before she could press hers.

What would the dolphins do? Dr. Bastian turned on the headlight and watched carefully. Doris stared at it. She looked at her buttons. Then she swam close to the wooden wall and began to whistle loudly. For a few seconds everything was quiet in the tank. Then Buzz whistled back, and pressed down one of his buttons. It was the correct one. Now Doris could press her button, and both dolphins would get their fish.

Again and again Dr. Bastian turned on the headlight. Sometimes it blinked. Sometimes it shone with a steady light. Each time Doris would look — and whistle. Then Buzz would press down the correct button on his side of the wall.

Was Doris telling Buzz what to do? Or was he just guessing? If so, Dr. Bastian thought, then Buzz was a wonderful guesser. He was right almost every time.

The Story of Zippy,
the blindfolded dolphin

Dolphins can hear very small noises under water. They can hear a pebble rolling. They can hear a fish gliding through a clump of sea grass. But what about things that don't make any noise at all — like a rock, or a sleeping fish? Scientists watched dolphins. And they noticed that dolphins seemed to know just where these silent things were too.

Did the dolphins use their eyes? Sometimes. Dolphins have very good eyesight. But sometimes at night the water was very dark. Sometimes it was filled with mud.

And the dolphins could still tell where everything was. They could tell things to swim toward — like fish. And things to swim away from — like rocks. Or sharks.

Scientists began to think that maybe dolphins were using more than their eyes to tell where everything was. They began to suspect that dolphins were also using sound to help them find out where things were.

The scientists noticed that sometimes dolphins made a very special sound. It was like a door swinging — a door with rusty hinges. The scientists thought that maybe this rusty hinge sound traveled through the water. It traveled until it bumped into something — a fish, a rock, a shark. Then the echo of this sound came bouncing back to the waiting dolphin. From this returning echo the dolphin built up a "picture" of the object in his mind. This round-trip of sound is called *sonar*.

The scientists thought that dolphins were using sonar to "see" in their water-world. But how could they be sure? A scientist named Dr. Kenneth Norris decided he would settle the question once and for all. He would blindfold a dolphin so that it could not see a thing. Would the dolphin still be able to tell where everything was?

But how do you blindfold a dolphin? This turned out to be quite a problem. Dr. Norris's dolphin was named Zippy. First Dr. Norris tried to put sponges over Zippy's eyes. He tried to hold them on with adhesive tape. But Zippy's skin was slippery and wet. No matter how much tape the doctor used, the sponges would not stick.

Next Dr. Norris tried earmuffs. The muffs were supposed to fit over Zippy's eyes. The band would circle her head. But the metal band came too close to her blow-hole — her nose. Zippy couldn't breathe. Earmuffs would not do.

Finally Dr. Norris tried rubber suction cups. And they worked the very first time! The cups clung gently to the skin around Zippy's eyes, and didn't hurt her at all.

At last! Dr. Norris and Zippy were ready for the big test. Dr. Norris planned to blow a whistle. When Zippy heard the whistle she was supposed to swim around the tank until she found an underwater lever. She was supposed to press it down. Then a bell would ring and she would get a reward — a piece of her favorite fish.

Zippy had already learned how to do this

— when she could see. But now she was blindfolded. Would she still be able to find the lever?

Dr. Norris blew his whistle. *Creee-eeeKKK*. Zippy turned her head from left to right and made her rusty hinge noise. Suddenly she swam off at high speed. She swam straight for the lever and gave it a good hard push!

But Dr. Norris was a scientist. And scientists have to be very, very sure. So again and again he put the lever in a different place. Again and again Zippy headed straight for it. The experiment was a complete success. Zippy, the blindfolded dolphin, was "seeing" with sonar.

The experiment was over. But before Dr. Norris said good-bye to Zippy he decided to try one more experiment. He wanted to block off Zippy's sonar. He wanted to prove that she would be helpless without it.

So he made a foam-rubber mask. The mask fitted over Zippy's snout and over the two earholes on top of her head. Dr. Norris was sure that when Zippy was wearing that mask she could creak and creak — and still not hear the tiniest echo of a returning sound.

Zippy seemed to think this was true too. She had always been a very easygoing dolphin. She had always been willing to do whatever Dr. Norris wanted her to do. But not now. Zippy refused to wear that mask. Again and again Dr. Norris slipped it over her head. Again and again Zippy shook her head until it fell off.

But Zippy didn't hold a grudge — even against this man who was giving her so

much trouble. Every time the mask fell to
the bottom of the tank, Zippy swam down
to it. She picked it up, and politely handed
it back to Dr. Norris!

The Story of Tuffy,
the dolphin who was trained to save lives

Everyone knows about astronauts — the men who explore outer space. Now people are beginning to hear more and more about aquanauts, the men who explore space under water.

In the fall of 1965 a group of aquanauts spent forty-five days under water near the coast of California. They were part of a project called Sealab II. One of the

58

aquanauts looked a little different from the others. No wonder. He was a three-hundred-pound dolphin named Tuffy.

Tuffy spent much of his time in a pen near the top of the water — so he could breathe. Home for the other aquanauts was a big metal capsule called Sealab which rested on the bottom of the ocean.

Every morning the human aquanauts put on their diving suits and left Sealab to swim in the water outside the capsule. They measured the underwater currents. They took pictures of the ocean floor. They put metal tags on the tails of some of the fish that swarmed around. They studied many different underwater plants.

Tuffy had jobs to do too. He had been trained to be a messenger. When he was working he wore a special harness. Waterproof bags could be hooked onto it. In those bags Tuffy carried mail and tools and sometimes medicines to the aquanauts below. Up, down, up, down, he swam — the only live link between two very different worlds.

Tuffy had been trained to do another job too. It was the most important of all. He had been trained to save lives.

The human aquanauts were safe inside Sealab. They had all sorts of comforts there — hot food, water, soft beds, books, even television. But the minute they stepped outside they entered a strange and dangerous world.

The sun often shone brightly on the top of the water. But it was always dark as night two hundred feet below, where the human aquanauts were exploring.

Each aquanaut carried two small tanks of

air on his back. That air meant the difference between life and death in this world of water. But what if an aquanaut got lost? What if he couldn't find his way back to the safety of Sealab before his air was used up?

The human aquanauts knew that if this happened they had one last hope. Tuffy. None of the men became lost during the Sealab II project. But they weren't taking any chances. Again and again they ran tests. They pretended to be lost.

A man would hide himself behind a rock or in the middle of a big clump of plants. He would set off a special buzzer he always carried with him. This buzzer could be heard on the surface of the water. "Emergency!" it meant. "A man is lost. We need Tuffy! Fast!"

Seconds later Tuffy would come plunging
down through the water. But he wouldn't

head for the "lost" aquanaut" — not right away. First he would swim to the Sealab capsule. He would slide his snout through a ring. The ring was attached to one end of a long rope. The other end of the rope was hooked to the metal side of Sealab.

Now *creee-eeeKKKKK*. Tuffy would scan the water with his sonar. Then off he'd swim toward the hiding man, trailing the rope behind him. Seconds later the man would take the ring from Tuffy. Now he could follow the lifeline of rope back to Sealab—and safety. And Tuffy? His job was done. So he would head for the top of the water for a welcome gulp of air.

Usually Tuffy made this round-trip of rescue in about one minute. Did he always do his job so quickly and so well? Yes... except once.

Tuffy was a very smart, very hard-working dolphin. But he was also stubborn. And he loved to eat. So when Tuffy brought the ring to an aquanaut he was always given a reward. Each man carried a small plastic bag of chopped fish. Tuffy would let the man take the ring. Then the man would squirt some fish into Tuffy's mouth.

But once something went wrong. The aquanaut tugged and tugged, but he couldn't get his bag of fish open. So finally he gave Tuffy a shove. "Move on," he meant.

But Tuffy didn't move on. *Where was his reward? Where was his mouthful of fish? This wasn't the way things were supposed to happen!* Tuffy stared at the man for a moment. He raised one of his flippers and bopped him over the head. *Then* the dolphin aquanaut swam on.